Original title:
Sprigs of Spirit

Copyright © 2025 Creative Arts Management OÜ
All rights reserved.

Author: Evan Hawthorne
ISBN HARDBACK: 978-1-80566-725-4
ISBN PAPERBACK: 978-1-80566-854-1

Serenity in Bloom

In the garden where giggles grow,
Pansies tell jokes to the tulips, you know.
With bees buzzing beats, they dance in a line,
Each petal a laugh, each stem a punchline.

In pots of old soil, dreams take a leap,
While daisies recite what the daisies keep.
A rose gives a wink, quite cheeky and bright,
As sunsets paint laughter in shades of delight.

Emerging from the Shadows

Out from the dark came a squirrel with flair,
Wearing a mask, he thought it quite rare.
He cracked a few nuts, made the branches shake,
Said, "Don't be so serious, for goodness' sake!"

In the moon's soft glow, a raccoon joined in,
With a top hat and tails, he twirled with a spin.
Together they giggled, casting away gloom,
As shadows became their comedic costume.

Cascades of Inner Wisdom

A waterfall chuckled, splashing with glee,
Gave wisecracks to fish all swimming carefree.
"What's the fish's favorite movie?" it crooned,
"Anything with a cast that's really well-tuned!"

With rocks that just rolled and moss that would tickle,
Every ripple of water would giggle and wiggle.
Nature's own classroom, laughter's big swell,
Where wisdom's a joke and all secrets tell.

Celestial Ferns of Emotion

In a forest of ferns where emotions run wild,
A tree whispered secrets, like a giddy child.
"What do you call a plant that's afraid of heights?"
"A lowly little fern with very short sights!"

With roots tangled up in a web of delight,
They tickled the ground, making harmony bright.
As laughter shot up through the branches so high,
The forest erupted with joy and a sigh.

The Essence Unfolds

In a garden of giggles, blooms brightly,
Laughter's perfume, oh so sprightly.
Petals tickle the nose, it's a show,
Squirrels in bow ties, putting on a glow.

Dandelions puff, like clouds on a whim,
Bees in a conga, their dance not so grim.
With every chuckle, the flowers all sway,
Tickled by breezes that play all day.

Roots of Reverie

Down in the soil, the roots throw a bash,
With worms in tuxedos, they shimmy and splash.
Earthworms whisper secrets, oh so profound,
As radishes plot to dig deep underground.

Carrots wear goggles to see the new day,
While cabbages craft their grand cabaret.
Underneath the moon, with laughter they weave,
A tale of mischief that none would believe.

Light Beneath the Canopy

Under a leafy roof, where shadows glow,
The critters converse, oh what a show!
With a squirrel on drums and a frog singing tune,
Even the lizards step out 'neath the moon.

Fireflies flicker, like lights gone awry,
Weaving tales of magic, a twinkling sky.
While owls hoot wisdom, with jokes on their tongue,
Laughter echoes through trees, forever young.

A Dance of Shadows

Shadows stretch long as the sun bids farewell,
While raccoons juggle acorns, oh can't you tell?
The twilight's a stage, for frogs to take flight,
As crickets compose serenades of delight.

In the dance of the dusk, all the critters unite,
With rabbits in top hats, it's a whimsical sight.
With every leap forward, they trip on their feet,
Embracing the joy in this quirky retreat.

Song of the Unseen

In the attic lives a ghost,
Who dances with an old toast.
He twirls in socks, two left feet,
And sings to the beat of a hamster's beat.

His friends include a savvy chair,
Who squeaks along without a care.
They chuckle loud at socks on high,
As shadows roll, they laugh and sigh.

A pumpkin sings a jolly tune,
On Halloween, they must be strewn.
With candy corn and jokes that flop,
They giggle till they nearly drop.

The broomstick winks, it knows the game,
Of silly fun and wild acclaim.
Around the house, a whirl of cheer,
Inspirations only ghosts hold dear.

Radiance in the Quiet

The light bulb flickers, what a mess,
It thinks it's cool, but it's just stressed.
In corners dark, it plays coy tricks,
While dust bunnies dance, seeking kicks.

A couch potato on a spree,
Claims victory in a snack-filled sea.
With chips as ships and dip for waves,
Lunch hour laughs, how it misbehaves.

While curtains flutter, a breeze so bold,
The tales of laughter, gaffes retold.
The cat looks on with sleepy eyes,
Plotting mischief in disguise.

And there, a sock hops with a jog,
Waving hello to its own dialogue.
In silence, echoes roar and tease,
Spirits giggle as they please.

Chasing The Whispering Winds

A breeze runs wild through the tall grass,
Whispering jokes as it does pass.
'Twas tickled by a passing kite,
Who begged for laughs through day and night.

The leaves traded puns with glee,
As squirrels chimed in, so carefree.
They spun tales of acorns lost,
And pondered if they'd pay the cost.

A dandelion donned a crown,
And strutted proudly through the town.
The honeybee buzzed, "What a show!"
"Just wait," said the wind, "There's more to blow!"

Around they twirled, a whimsical dance,
While the sun peered down, giving a glance.
And every gust brought giggles bright,
In the chase for laughter, pure delight.

Tapestry of Tides

The waves come in with a cheeky grin,
Splashing at shore like a playful kin.
They whisper secrets to the sand,
And giggle at shells that don't understand.

A crab in sunglasses struts with flair,
While starfish ponder with little care.
"Why be a star when you can be a crab?"
The ocean chuckles, it's soft and fab.

Seagulls squawk with a wink, it seems,
As they dive for fish and join in dreams.
With each tide rising, laughter rolls,
Creating waves to soothe our souls.

In salty air, the whispers grow,
Of mermaid tales and seaweed shows.
For in the tides, where giggles reside,
Life's a funny ride, we won't hide!

Whispers of the Wild

In the forest, squirrels chat,
About the latest nutty spat.
Trees eavesdrop, leaves in a swirl,
As branches dance, the wildlife twirl.

Frogs croak jokes in muddy ponds,
While shy raccoons plot their fronds.
Wisdom's found in playful jest,
What a hoot to be nature's guest!

Bunnies hop with a wink and smile,
Sharing secrets all the while.
In the wild, laughter runs free,
Just a hush from a buzzing bee.

So listen close to the rustling sound,
Nature's laughter all around.
In the whispers of the great outdoors,
Find joy that endlessly pours.

Embers of the Soul

A campfire crackles with crackpot tales,
As marshmallows toast on wobbly trails.
Ghosts of laughter float in the night,
S'mores and giggles, what a delight!

Old socks heat up with playfully schtick,
Charred hot dogs? Just a little thick.
Beneath the stars, the stories spin,
Add a spark, let the fun begin!

Fireflies dance like tiny light bulbs,
Playing games, doing their own jigs and wobbles.
The night hums with a joyful tune,
While shadows join in a silly swoon.

So let the flames flicker and gleam,
In funny moments, let's all dream.
These embers glow brighter with every bold jest,
In the warmth of laughter, we find our rest.

Echoes in the Breeze

A gentle gust whispers, "Hey, all aboard!"
While leaves play tag and the sun can't be ignored.
Grasshoppers chirp with a comedic flair,
While dandelions fluff up their crazy hair.

Clouds drift lazily, not a worry in sight,
Swapping jokes as they float through the light.
The wind carries secrets with each soft sigh,
As birds laugh together, flapping up high.

Breezes curl around, tickling your nose,
Reminding you how each giggle grows.
In the air, hues of silly collide,
With echoes of joy that cannot subside.

So next time the zephyr invites you to play,
Join in the laughter come what may.
Together we ride on whimsical dreams,
In the giggling whispers, joy brightly beams.

Petals of Resilience

Blossoms giggle as they open wide,
Dancing about in the morning tide.
Petals flutter with a cheeky grin,
"Bloom where you're planted, let the fun begin!"

Sunshine tickles each flower's face,
While bees take selfies at a quick pace.
Dandelions yell, "We're wild and free!"
Spreading laughter over the whole marquee.

Tulips wear hats made of dew,
Strutting their stuff, a floral review.
"Come one, come all, the show's about,"
In gardens alive with a jubilant shout.

So when life pulls you into a strife,
Remember the petals that dance with life.
In every whimsy, find joy and persistence,
For laughter's the heart of true existence.

Pockets of Radiance

In my pocket, a sunbeam hides,
A cheeky glow that gently bides.
It giggles when I reach to peek,
"You've found me now!" it starts to speak.

A dance of light, a twinkling cheer,
With every step, it wobbles near.
It tickles toes and leaps with glee,
This silly glow, it loves to be free.

I take it out to show a friend,
But in the breeze, it starts to bend.
"Catch me quick!" it plays a trick,
And vanishes with a comical flick.

Now every pocket holds a surprise,
A tiny star that loves to rise.
So if you hear a glinting laugh,
Check your coat, you might find the path!

Gentle Roots of Joy

In the garden of my happy heart,
There's a plant that loves to play its part.
With roots that wiggle in the ground,
It spreads giggles all around.

The leaves wear hats, a colorful show,
Each one ready for a fun-filled throw.
They wave at bees with a wobbly grin,
"Come join us, let's begin!"

A ticklish breeze makes them sway,
They dance and twirl at break of day.
"Isn't life a jolly jam?"
They shout, while munching on some spam.

And when the morn begins to fade,
The roots still craft their silly parade.
With laughter sprinkled in the soil,
They spread delight as they softly toil!

Hidden Petals of Light

In the thicket where secrets sway,
Petals hide and play all day.
They whisper jokes to passing bees,
And giggle softly with the trees.

Each blossom's got a punchline bright,
They bloom with laughter, pure delight.
"Why did the flower break apart?"
"To petal faster, sweet like tart!"

They're shy and fierce, a silly mix,
With shining hues, they love their tricks.
When clouds roll in, they shiver, play,
"Come dance with us before the gray!"

So if you wander through the brush,
You might just hear a laughing hush.
For hidden petals, bold and spry,
Know how to twinkle, wink, and fly!

Swaying in the Margins

In the margins where the wild things peek,
There's a crew of whimsies, oh so sleek.
They sway and giggle, out of sight,
Impromptu performers in the twilight.

One juggles acorns, a real hoot,
While others dance in orange boots.
They sing of mischief, playful pride,
As shadows stretch, they come alive.

With every rustle, they hum a tune,
Tickled by the light of the moon.
"This world's our stage!" they cheer, so loud,
As tiny wonders gather round.

Swaying in the Margins

In the margins where the wild things peek,
There's a crew of whimsies, oh so sleek.
They sway and giggle, out of sight,
Impromptu performers in the twilight.

One juggles acorns, a real hoot,
While others dance in orange boots.
They sing of mischief, playful pride,
As shadows stretch, they come alive.

With every rustle, they hum a tune,
Tickled by the light of the moon.
"This world's our stage!" they cheer, so loud,
As tiny wonders gather round.

The Heart's Garden

In the garden where giggles bloom,
Silly squirrels dance in a plume.
With flowers that tickle and tease,
They sway in the breeze with great ease.

The daisies wear hats made of cheese,
While bees buzz around, aiming to please.
The sunflowers joke with the sun,
Claiming their laughter is never done.

A garden gnome cracks the wildest puns,
His jokes sprouting like popcorn runs.
In this quirky patch of delight,
Every leaf has a story to write.

So come, grab a weed or a hoe,
Join the laughter, let the joy flow.
For in this garden, we plant our cheer,
Growing giggles that echo all year.

Threads of the Untamed

In a world where socks don't quite match,
And cats wear ties, quite the catch.
They pounce on threads that twirl and spin,
Creating chaos, with cheeky grins.

A dog in a bonnet struts down the lane,
While hedgehogs play chess in the rain.
With notions unraveled and yarn gone wild,
Each tangled snip brings laughter unfiled.

The midges wear boots, ready to stomp,
As caterpillars gather for a romp.
In a tapestry stitched with glee,
Life's threads intertwine, wild and free.

So spin the yarn, let the mischief unfurl,
In patterns of joy, we twirl and swirl.
For in the fabric of jest we find,
The threads of delight, beautifully twined.

Fluttering Memories

A butterfly flops with a flair,
Wearing a hat, what a sight to share!
It bumps into daisies in a lark,
Spreading nostalgia, hitting its mark.

A tickled sparrow hums a tune,
While a snail dons shades, looking like a boon.
Memories flutter on wings of delight,
Reminding us all of carefree nights.

Down by the brook, the fish wear smiles,
As frogs in tuxedos get into styles.
Each splash a giggle, a laugh that can sing,
In the pool of remembrance, joy is the king.

So lift up your chin and let laughter fly,
For memories wink under the sky.
With every flutter, a story unfolds,
In the tapestry of life, it's laughter that holds.

The Lilt of Living

In the dance of the day, let's sway and spin,
Where laughter bubbles like a fizzy gin.
With shoelaces tangled, we trip and fall,
But joy is the net that catches us all.

The trees wear glasses, looking so wise,
While rabbits bake cookies, a sweet surprise.
Under the moon's silly grin so bright,
We celebrate living — what a delight!

With each wobbly step, a twirl or a leap,
We find humor tucked in pockets so deep.
In the rhythm of life, let's jig and prance,
For even the clumsy can share in the dance.

So laugh at the mess and giggle with glee,
In the lilt of living — oh can't you see?
Each moment a jest, a joyful refrain,
In our funny little world, let's be a bit insane.

Blossoms of Resilience

In the garden of wits, a bloom does tease,
Chasing the bees, while sipping on cheese.
Petals are giggling, oh what a sight!
Swaying to rhythms all day and all night.

Dancing in laughter as storms come and go,
Hiding in shadows, then putting on a show.
Roots are all tangled, a comedic clasp,
With every twist fighting to catch their gasp.

Leaves wear sunglasses, looking so fine,
Chilling with daisies and sipping on wine.
Nature's a jester, with puns to unearth,
In the soil of humor, we find our true worth.

Buds burst with joy, they jump and they bop,
Sharing the jokes that never do stop.
Life's a wild punchline, a giggle parade,
In the heart of the garden, laughter won't fade.

Vines of Vigor

Climbing the fence, with a sly little grin,
These vines have no limits, they just love to win.
Twirling and swirling, a show of great flair,
Pulling in the sun, with style so rare.

They wrap around raindrops and ride on the breeze,
Sprouting wild stories that bring us to ease.
With every new knot, a punchline's unveiled,
In the tangled embrace, no laughter's curtailed.

Foliage flaunts in a playful parade,
Bouncing and flopping, like jokes that won't fade.
Nature's comedians, in green they reside,
Mischief in every leaf, so spryly they glide.

So let's raise a cheer for the light-hearted vines,
For laughter's the harvest, where joy intertwines.
They wave their green arms, in jest and delight,
Giving us smiles from morning to night.

Essence in the Breeze

A whisper of joy floats past in the air,
Tickling the nostrils, a scent beyond compare.
Caught in a chuckle, the wind starts to sway,
Bringing in giggles that frolic and play.

Leaves rustle secrets, shared between friends,
Jokes on the branches, where laughter transcends.
Each gust's a punchline, tickling the trees,
In this wacky world, where humor's a breeze.

Sunshine is beaming, wearing a crown,
Dancing with flowers, never a frown.
Bees buzzing laughter, on their merry quest,
In this whimsical realm, we're really the best.

So inhale the giggles and let your heart soar,
For mirth in the air always opens the door.
Nature's punchlines, without any tease,
Sprinkling joy in the essence of breeze.

Green Threads of Vitality

Stitched with humor, these threads intertwine,
Binding together the silly and fine.
Woven in laughter, a tapestry bright,
Each stitch a joke, bringing warmth and delight.

Grass blades are chuckling, as folks step on through,
Tickling toes with their green, fresh debut.
A canvas of giggles, beneath every toe,
In the quilt of the earth where joy tends to grow.

Fronds wave and wink, with a cheeky flair,
Knitting up puns in the soft, fragrant air.
Laughter's the fabric that holds us so tight,
In the quilt of existence where everything's right.

So come wrap yourself in this greenery bright,
Where the threads of good humor will spark your delight.

For in every fiber lies giggles and cheer,
Where playful spirits gather and draw ever near.

Celestial Currents

In the sky, a flying fish,
Wears a hat that's quite delish.
Stars giggle in their sparkling dance,
While comets twirl in cosmic pants.

Jupiter's got a giant grin,
As aliens play a jazz violin.
Saturn's rings are jumping high,
Like a hula hoop that's far too shy.

A cloud shapes up into a dog,
Chasing rainbows lost in fog.
Planets spin, throwing a bash,
Galactic fun, make a splash!

With laughter echoing through the night,
Even asteroids join in the delight.
They tumble, giggle—what a sight!
In this space of whimsy, all feels right.

Fragments of Elysium

In Eden's land of quirk and jest,
The apples glow, but who knows best?
A serpent's tongue, oh what a tease,
While fairies giggle 'round the trees.

Peacocks strut with feathery flair,
Dancing like they just don't care.
Napping clouds drift by so slow,
Snoring softly, putting on a show.

Lemons laugh as they roll down hills,
Chasing butterflies with tiny thrills.
A garden party hosted by bees,
With honey cakes and a buzz of glee.

Grapes play tag, rushing with glee,
While sunflowers sip on herbal tea.
In this land where laughter reigns,
Joy's the cure for all life's pains.

Beneath the Serene Sky

Under bright, fluffy clouds of cream,
A puppy wakes from a silly dream.
Chasing its tail with endless zest,
Wiggling around, it's truly blessed.

Balloons float high, a colorful flight,
Pigs with wings delight in their height.
Kites are tangled in a dance of mirth,
As giggles echo, filling the Earth.

Caterpillars spin tales on a leaf,
While ladybugs chuckle, devoid of grief.
Insects waltz under moonlit beams,
Unraveling the fabric of our dreams.

Mirth like sunshine warms the ground,
Every critter wears a crown.
Beneath this vast, enchanted dome,
We find a world we're proud to roam.

The Bloom of Being

In a garden where laughter grows,
Jokes bloom bright like a pretty rose.
Dandelions giggle, all aglow,
Spreading cheer with every blow.

A squirrel flips on a swing of pine,
Chasing bees as they sip on wine.
Bunnies hop in bizarre ballet,
Swinging their ears in a silly way.

Mushrooms sport tops, polka-dotted glee,
While worms groove like they're at a spree.
Each petal's adorned with a merry grin,
Celebrating the joy that lives within.

Time ticks slowly, smiles take flight,
In this bloom, everything feels right.
Join the whirls, the silly show,
In nature's heart, let laughter flow!

Echoes of the Soul

In the garden of giggles, we dance,
Whispers of jest take their chance,
A squirrel in a suit with a top hat,
Wiggling his tail, how cool is that?

Under the shade of a laughing tree,
Its branches sway, so carefree,
The flowers chuckle in bright hues,
Throwing petals like confetti in queues.

Bumblebees buzz, a musical band,
Playing tunes on their tiny stand,
While daisies sport their sunny grins,
As if they know all the world's sins.

Each echo rings with a hearty laugh,
Sharing secrets on life's quirky path,
In this silly patch of vibrant cheer,
The soul finds joy, year after year.

Lush Tendrils of Hope

A vine climbed high, what a sight,
Wearing a crown of leaves so light,
It tickled the clouds, oh such fun,
Chatting with birds 'til the day was done.

On the ground, a frog sings loud,
In a bowtie, he feels so proud,
With a croak that's heard all around,
In muddy waters, he's glory-bound.

Each leaf whispers a wish, you see,
Like little thoughts that dance with glee,
Spinning dreams like webs from a spider,
While laughing at woes, getting brighter.

Hope tumbles down from branches above,
Covered in laughter and loads of love,
An amusement park for the weary heart,
Where each little jest plays its part.

Fragrant Echoes of Growth

A plant wakes up with a yawn and stretch,
It spotted its neighbor, a cactus sketch,
With spiky jokes and a prickly grin,
Challenging all to a laughter spin.

Marigolds bloom with a sunny cheer,
Their petals flutter like jokes in the air,
As dew drops giggle on the green ground,
Marching with joy, all around, all around.

The sun spills honey over the scene,
Toasting each sprout in a bright sheen,
Roots of humor delving deep in the earth,
Springing forth laughter, a joyous rebirth.

Growth is a giggle, a raucous delight,
Every leaf a comic, twinkling bright,
In this garden where whimsy is king,
The echoes of joy are what we bring.

Subtle Hues of Harmony

In a rainbow of chuckles, colors collide,
Where blues waddle and reds like to slide,
Purple giggles as it leaps and bounds,
In this colorful world, laughter resounds.

From the grasshopper's hop to the butterfly's twirl,
Every tiny creature gives life a whirl,
A symphony sung in giggles and grins,
Revealing the joy that harmony wins.

Trees sway gently in a comical dance,
As wind whispers jokes with a light glance,
Each leaf a note in a playful song,
Where even the shy ones just join along.

In subtle hues that tickle the heart,
Harmony plays its bright, quirky part,
Life's canvas painted with chuckles and mirth,
In the laughter of harmony, we find our worth.

Petals of the Forgotten

In a garden once bright, a flower forgot,
Told a joke to a bee, but it flew off a lot.
The daisies all chuckled, the tulips turned red,
While the roses just sighed, 'Now that's what I said!'

With petals a-flutter, they started a game,
'Who can shout loudest without feeling lame?'
The clovers grew anxious, their voices went shy,
But the dandelions laughed, 'We can all touch the sky!'

A gnome in the corner began to dance too,
He slipped on a leaf, and fell right in the dew.
The laughter echoed, as the sun took a peek,
And the nightingales chirped, 'Now this is our week!'

So join in the fun, with laughter to share,
Amidst blooms of the past, our joy fills the air.
In gardens where petals once secretly hid,
It's a party of blooms, oh, what fun they all did!

Clusters of Renewal

In a patch of green leaves, a squirrel found snacks,
He giggled and danced while avoiding the cracks.
Gathering joy from each acorn he found,
Proclaimed to the trees, 'I am truly renowned!'

A rabbit joined in, with a hop and a skip,
Said, 'What's in your stash? Let's start a fun trip!'
They planned the great feast, to eat nuts and greens,
While sharing their dreams of springtime routines.

As the sun started shining, they threw a wild bash,
Dancing with daisies, and singing quite brash.
With a juggling act of ripe fruit from a vine,
Their laughter rang out, oh, what a good time!

So if you feel down and want to renew,
Just find a bunch of pals and bring them with you.
Together you'll sparkle with laughter and cheer,
In clusters of friendship, the good times are near!

Mellow Waves of Spirit

On a beach made of grass, where the breezes do flow,
A parrot named Pete put on quite the show.
With a wink and a squawk, he danced on the sand,
Pretending he was in a big rock band.

The crabs started clapping their claws in delight,
While the turtles brought snacks, a truly grand sight.
They laughed at the waves that tickled their toes,
As the jellyfish jived, in mismatched pink clothes.

A seagull sang high, but was off-key and loud,
While the ocean just chuckled, under a cloud.
Yet all joined the fun, in the colorful breeze,
With each fellow creature doing just as they please.

So if you seek joy in soft blankets of blue,
Just sway with the breeze, and dance like you do.
In mellow good vibes where the laughter can soar,
Every wave brings a smile that you can't help but roar!

The Language of Leaves

In a whispering grove, the leaves spoke a tune,
They chatted of squirrels and danced 'neath the moon.
With each rustle and shake, they shared little tales,
Like a gossiping creek, full of fun and of gales.

One leaf said, 'Listen! I just saw a frog,
He slipped on a lily, oh what a big slog!'
They giggled together, a chorus of green,
'Frogs in such gowns, oh the sights we've all seen!'

As fireflies flickered, they started to plan,
A big leafy party, a celebration grand.
With acorns and twigs, they made hats and balloons,
Laughing so hard, they woke up the raccoons.

So next time you wander through trees that you see,
Stop close and just listen, join in their glee.
For leaves have a language, all fun, joy, and jest,
In this world of wonders, you're surely a guest!

Tresses of Tranquility

In a garden where giggles grow,
Plants itch for a tickle, don't you know?
A lettuce made a pun, it's true,
Spilling salad jokes — oh, what a view!

The daisies danced with a silly sway,
While the carrot told stories of yesterday.
They whispered secrets in the dew,
Of how to sprout laughter like morning brew.

Bubbly buds, they spritz and cheer,
Throwing petals, spreading good cheer.
In this patch of laughter, they unite,
With jokes that bloom from morning till night.

Nurtured by the Earth

Worms wiggle in their earthy beds,
Planning pranks before they're fed.
A thistle cracks jokes, sharp and bold,
While mushrooms share tales of the old.

The soil's a stage, nature's delight,
Where ants perform in the pale moonlight.
With beetles playing drums in a band,
All nature's quirks go hand in hand.

Each droplet dances, a wink and a nudge,
Even rocks know how to grudge.
In this funky patch, all's a jest,
Laughter tucked in with nature's rest.

Dancing with the Winds

The breeze tickles leaves with a cheeky grin,
As twirling branches join in the spin.
A squirrel, all fluffy, attempts a leap,
While the winds blow secrets it can't keep.

They laugh as they swirl, a wild ballet,
Chasing each other, come what may.
A cloud rolls in, the joker of gas,
Pouring laughter like rain, oh, what a class!

Twists and turns, they swirl around,
In an aerial giggle, nature's sound.
Every gust holds a joke or two,
In this dance where skies feel brand new.

Vibrant Embers of Being

Funky flames flicker, all dressed up,
Sipping on laughter from a giant cup.
With sparks that crackle at every jest,
They spread joy, making the night zest.

Each ember wiggles, trying to dance,
While shadows giggle at their glance.
"Keep it bright!" they shout with cheer,
As laughter illuminates all that's near.

The fireflies blink, playing tag with light,
In this fiery chaos, everything's right.
With warmth and chuckles that fill the air,
Even the night can't help but stare.

The Pulse of Nature's Heart

In gardens where the daisies dance,
The squirrels sing a silly prance.
They hide their acorns, what a sight,
While dreaming of a nutty bite.

The bees are buzzing, wearing hats,
In tiny suits, those little brats.
They sip on nectar, throw a ball,
And hold a party, one and all.

The flowers gossip, secrets shared,
About the sun and how it dared.
To shine so bright, it made them swoon,
Underneath the laughing moon.

So dance along, you merry crew,
In nature's realm, there's fun for you.
With every heartbeat, giggles burst,
As joy in blooms is truly versed.

Vistas of Renewal

In springs that tickle daffodil,
The frogs wear ties and strike a chill.
With croaks like jazz, they leap about,
As if the world's a funny route.

The streams are giggling, bubbling bright,
Reflecting clouds in a slapstick flight.
Fish in top hats swim with flair,
While turtles ponder, 'Why this wear?'

Blossoms burst in colors bold,
As butterflies spin tales retold.
In every petal, laughter's found,
As nature's pranksters gather 'round.

So join the mischief, let it soar,
With joy and laughter at its core.
In every breeze and bloom we see,
A world of whimsy, wild and free.

Seeds of Serendipity

Once I planted a tiny seed,
What grew was quite a funny breed.
A beanstalk sprouted, big and round,
That wore a hat and danced unbound.

The daisies played a game of tag,
While bunnies wore a classic rag.
They tripped and fell in joyful heaps,
As laughter echoed through the creeps.

The sun peeked in with a cheeky grin,
While rain clouds wondered where to begin.
A rainbow formed a bridge to fun,
Connecting worlds till day was done.

So plant a seed of silly seeds,
And watch the growth of joyful deeds.
In every sprout, the laughter grows,
In nature's whims, the joy bestows.

Symphony of the Unseen

In hidden realms where shadows play,
The crickets hold a cabaret.
With tiny violins they croon,
Beneath the smiling cheeky moon.

The rustling leaves join in the fun,
Swaying dancers, one by one.
A breeze conducts this wacky show,
As fireflies put on quite the glow.

The nightingale adds rhymes and jests,
While all the critters take their rests.
With chuckles wrapped in soft night air,
They spin their tales without a care.

So turn up the volume, join the spree,
With nature's tune, a jubilee.
In every note, a giggle's found,
In this wild symphony, we're all unbound.

Cascading Petals of Discovery

In a garden so bright, I took a trip,
To find flowers that dance and sometimes slip.
They giggle and sway like they're in a show,
Spreading secrets of joy with each little blow.

I met a bee dressed in tiny green pants,
Who buzzed all around, insisting on chance.
He whispered of nectar, so sweet, oh so fine,
With a wink and a twirl, he asked if I'd dine.

Petals were leaping, oh what a delight,
As they swirled in the breeze, like confetti in flight.
I grabbed a bouquet, but got chased by a bee,
Turns out he just wanted to share his sweet tea!

With laughter and blooms, the day came to close,
I skipped through the fields, fresh flowered toes.
If you ever feel down, just take a quick trip,
To the garden of antics, where nature won't slip.

Nature's Gentle Affirmation

The trees shake their leaves, it's a comedic show,
With branches that sway, putting on quite a flow.
They wink and they nod, as if in a pact,
That nature's big party's got just the right act.

A squirrel with a hat and a bowtie on tight,
Decided to breakdance under the moonlight.
He flipped and he flopped, fell straight on his back,
Then laughed at his blunders, no confidence lack.

The birds joined the chorus, off-key but so proud,
Singing songs about nuts, as they gathered a crowd.
Nature stood tall, offering cheer with each sound,
Reminding us all, that joy's all around.

With giggles and grins, the night wrapped its arms,
And promised tomorrow, more nature-filled charms.
So join in the ruckus, parade with a smile,
In this festival of life, come stay for a while.

Vital Threads of Connection

In a world made of fibers and silly old dreams,
I found a grand spider weaving wild seams.
He spun tales of friendship with a delicate thread,
While I laughed at his hat, made of leaves, green and red.

The ants held a meeting, quite down on the floor,
Debating which crumb was deserving of more.
With tiny little gestures, they caused quite the fuss,
Waving their arms like an enthusiastic bus!

A butterfly waltzed, covering ground oh so wide,
Bragging about travels, quite full of pride.
He said, "Life's a journey, you never know when,
You'll find a warm flower or a spam email then!"

So let's connect with laughter, it's free, please don't scoff,

To the buzzing of nature, let's all take a soft off.
With threads of delight binding our hearts, oh so sweet,
Life's humor and love, we'll always repeat!

Budding Echoes of the Soul

In the morning, a bud whispered tales of the night,
Of dreams that took flight, oh what a delight!
It giggled at sunlight, tickled its toes,
Then stretched out its petals, saying, 'See how it goes!'

A gopher in shades was out for a stroll,
Claiming that sunshine's the ultimate goal.
He waved at the daisies who shook with a cheer,
Singing 'Don't worry! The fun's always near!'

A ladybug passed, with her spots in a row,
Proclaiming her wisdom, with a confident glow.
"Don't fret about things, just dance in the rain,
Life's polish comes best when it's wild and insane!"

With echoes of laughter, the garden did bloom,
Filling the air with a whimsical boom.
So take a deep breath, let humor be the goal,
For every small chuckle's a budding of soul!

Flourishing in the Quiet

In the silence, whispers grow,
A tumbleweed's dance, just so.
Socks and sandals, quite the pair,
A garden thriving without a care.

Napping gnomes under shady trees,
While daisies gossip in the breeze.
The sun beaming with a cheeky wink,
Chasing shadows, who'd even think?

Puddles reflect a sunny grin,
While worms do yoga, stretching thin.
The peaceful creek hums a tune,
With frogs joining in a silly croon.

A snail races, oh what a sight!
Waving slowly—what a delight!
In the quiet, laughter's found,
Sprouting joy from the ground.

Wellspring of Inner Light

Within us flows a quirky stream,
Where unicorns play, living the dream.
They sip on rainbows, oh so bright,
Bouncing off clouds like pure delight.

A giggle hides behind a tree,
While squirrels plot mischief with glee.
The moon serves cookies late at night,
Under stars, what a silly sight!

Wisdom grows under wild hats,
As raccoons share secrets with chatty bats.
In the garden of our minds,
The wittiest of treasures we find.

A parrot squawks a joke or two,
While sleepwalkers dance in muddy shoes.
In the hum of life, chuckles bloom,
In this wellspring, joy makes room.

Wildflowers of the Heart

In fields where giggles twist and twirl,
A bee teases flowers, giving a whirl.
With polka dots on petals bright,
Bumblebees ballet in pure delight.

Dandelions chuckle as they spread,
Their fluffy wishes float overhead.
A tulip trips on its own two feet,
Stumbling over chirps—truly sweet!

Butterflies wear spectacles of style,
As ladybugs waltz with a wink and a smile.
In this patch, all stories start,
Each bloom a tale, a work of art.

When the breeze plays hide and seek,
Petals shimmy, so to speak.
In the splatter of color, laughter departs,
Wildflowers thriving in our hearts.

Vibrant Chords of Existence

In the symphony of morning dew,
A rooster croons to a spunky crew.
Chickens jam with a funny beat,
Tap-dancing with their little feet.

Caterpillars strum on leaves so green,
They've formed a band, if you know what I mean!
Fireflies glow, lighting up the night,
While owls hoot a tune in flight.

Raccoons play tambourine, what a show!
While mushrooms groove, putting on a glow.
In this chorus, laughter abounds,
Life's lively rhythm continually sounds.

So let's join in, with a silly dance,
Embracing each moment, give life a chance.
In the vibrant chords, we find our song,
Where joy strums loudly, all day long.

Luminous Footprints

In the mud, I lost my shoe,
But now it glows—a neon hue.
Who knew my foot could shine so bright?
I dance like crazy, what a sight!

My left foot says, "Look at me!"
The right one screams, "I want to be!"
They wiggle, jiggle, all around,
I'm the funniest sight in town!

My dog just stares, like, 'What's this?'
He sniffs the glow, adds to the bliss.
A glowing foot parade in sync,
We're just a pair of fools, I think!

So here I go, ten toes aglow,
With hindsight proving I'm no pro.
Next time, I'll stick to rubber shoes,
But hey, at least I've got some views!

Enchantment in the Stillness.

In the garden, fairies play,
They hide my keys each sunny day.
I search high and I search low,
But giggles hide where no one goes.

The bees join in, they laugh so sweet,
As I trip over my own two feet.
With flowers whispering their delight,
My morning dance turns into flight!

A gnome rolls by, all out of shape,
He says, "Trust me, I'm an escape!"
But all he does is wiggle away,
I laugh so hard, I nearly sway.

As dusk arrives, they all retreat,
I'm left alone with my bare feet.
But tales of silliness remain,
I'll never see my keys again!

Whispers of Renewal

A squirrel's got a shining hat,
It's made of leaves and looks quite fat.
With acorns tucked beneath his chin,
He struts around, a little king!

He declares, "I'm off to fame!"
While the birds just shrug and stake their claim.
They laugh and chirp, "What a sight!"
As his fashion pride takes flight.

He winks at me, and off he flies,
My coffee spills, I nearly cry!
His crown so grand, it catches eyes,
A rodent now in fashion highs.

Yet in the morning, what a switch!
He's but a bum, not a rich niche.
Now just a critter, bare and free,
His hat's for sale—was that just me?

Flourishing Fragments

In my pot, a cactus grew,
It's prickly, yet it waved to you.
With tiny arms, it beckons me,
I'm not the one to shake, you see!

A sunflower tried to start a chat,
But got distracted with a hat.
It wore the sun, what a delight,
Chasing shadows left and right.

The daisies joined in with a dance,
They twirled around as if by chance.
I took a step and fell right down,
Laughter echoed all around town.

So here I sit, a messy sight,
With flowers giggling, pure delight.
In this wild garden, all absurd,
I've never felt so simply stirred!

Harmonies of the Heart

In the garden of giggles, we dance with glee,
Singing silly songs, just you and me.
A whoopee cushion plays a melody,
As starlit wishes float, wild and free.

With a wink and a nudge, we chase away blues,
Tickles abound, who needs a snooze?
Jokes bloom like flowers, bright and absurd,
Laughter is music, haven't you heard?

Through snickers and snorts, the joy never wanes,
In this comedy club, no one has chains.
With hearts full of mirth, we're ever so clever,
Crafting a life that's light as a feather.

So let's prance through the fields, where silliness reigns,
Chasing the clouds as we hop on the trains.
In this carnival spirit, may we never depart,
For laughter's the rhythm, the joy of the heart.

Tapestry of the Untamed

In the jungle of chuckles, where laughter runs wild,
A lion in slippers prances, oh so styled.
Monkeys play banjos, a band gone astray,
While parrots squawk jokes, come join in the play!

Amidst tangled vines, we craft a great feast,
Bamboo plates filled with pie, oh what a beast!
The elephant struts, in a tutu he wears,
Making everyone giggle, yes, by all means, cheers!

The hippos in hats are a sight to behold,
Rolling in laughter, their antics so bold.
Each creature adds charm to this merry parade,
In a riot of fun, not a moment to fade.

So swing from the branches and jump off the ground,
In this untamed realm, let hilarity abound.
With a wink to the wise and a grin for the young,
Join the tapestry woven, where jokes are well-spun.

Aurora of Inner Reflection

At dawn's early light, we stumble and grin,
With bedhead like lions and breakfast to win.
Coffee spills over, a mocha cascade,
As we share our dreams, both goofy and staid.

Waking like sloths, moving slow as a snail,
In mismatched socks, we're off on a trail.
The sunrise pulls pranks, painting skies with delight,
As shadows dance foolishly, outsmarting the light.

In the mirror's reflection, we wink and we pose,
With faces of feather, and giggles that grows.
Contemplating greatness while tripping on shoes,
What wisdom we gather, nobody can lose!

So let's toast to mornings, bright and absurd,
To waffles with laughter, and tea cups that curd!
Embrace the reflections, let joy be the guide,
In the aurora of life, where silliness hides.

Inflorescence of Dreams

In a meadow of thoughts where wild wishes sprout,
We plant silly seeds of a giggling sprout.
With whimsical whispers carried by breeze,
Dreams bloom in colors that tickle and tease.

Dancing through daisies, our imaginations run,
With pancakes in pockets and ice cream for fun.
The trees tell us stories, all grown up from seeds,
As we chase down the rainbows, collecting our leads.

Each night, we weave tales of gnomes and knights,
With capes made of laughter and paper kite flights.
So let's build a castle with clouds as our door,
And have tea with a walrus, who's never a bore.

In this garden of antics, our spirits take flight,
With fingernails painted in sparkles so bright.
Let dreams be delicious, with fudge on the side,
In this playful inflorescence, let joy be our guide.

Leaves of Living Essence

In the garden of giggles, I found quite a mess,
A cabbage patch kid in a lettuce dress.
Beetroot blushes, oh what a sight,
Dancing with carrots in the moonlight.

The peas are plotting a green little coup,
While radishes laugh at their own silly hue.
Tomatoes are tickled, they squirt and they spray,
As onions just cry, and wish they could play.

A pumpkin once tried to be scary and bold,
But tripped on a turnip, and that story's gold.
It rolled down the hill with a comedic flair,
As zucchinis chuckled and joined in the dare.

So here in this patch of whimsical glee,
Nature knows well how to make us agree.
Let's laugh with the veggies, in fun we'll reside,
For life's a big salad, let's toss it with pride.

Embraced by the Earth

In the soil's warm hug, I found a sweet joy,
A worm doing ballet, what a curious ploy!
The daisies are gossiping stories so grand,
While daisies are holding a flower parade band.

The daisies have dressed for the grand old fête,
While bees hum the tunes that they're trying to create.
A lily can't stop with her winks and her giggles,
As she sways in the breeze and performs funny wiggles.

Ants march by proudly, with crumbs on display,
They think they're the kings of this earthy buffet.
But a ladybug lands, with a wink and a spin,
Declaring a party where everyone wins!

So let's celebrate dirt, and the fun that it brings,
With worms and with flowers, and all tiny things.
Life's a wild romp, in earth's warm embrace,
Embracing the chaos with laughter and grace.

A Symphony of Color

In the meadow of hues where the sunlight does dance,
The flowers say, 'Join us! Let's have a prance!'
The violets giggle, the sunflowers spin,
While roses do cartwheels, with thorns tucked in.

The orange blooms blare, like trumpets so loud,
While bluebells whisper, 'We're feeling quite proud'.
Dandelions' wishes float high in the air,
While clovers play poker without any care.

Lilies are swaying with charming chic flair,
Each petal a rhythm, so lively and rare.
A rainbow's in chorus, a visual pie,
As nature composes beneath the wide sky.

So laugh with the flowers, let's share in the song,
For each hue is bright, where we all belong.
In this garden of giggles, we find our own tune,
A kaleidoscope symphony beneath the full moon.

Tangles of Wisdom

In the thicket of thoughts where the wild things go,
A squirrel with spectacles says, 'Watch me, now flow!'
He spins tales of acorns and games played up high,
While chattering birds join with a laugh and a sigh.

The wise old owl, with a grin that could bake,
Advises on branches, 'Don't make such a mistake!'
'For life's a good riddle, with quirks if you see,
Just roll with the punches, like leaves on a tree.'

The wise turtles giggle, and share their own games,
While rabbits recite their most ridiculous names.
Each whisper of wind carries wisdom so clear,
And laughter erupts for all nature to hear.

So come gather 'round, in this wild jubilance,
Let's spin our best stories, let our spirits dance!
In tangles of laughter, with friends big and small,
We find the deep wisdom that's fun for us all.

Ebb and Flow of the Heart

In the dance of socks, I find my match,
A woeful waltz with my laundry batch.
My heart does skip with every fold,
Like a game of twister, or so I'm told.

A spark ignites when my toaster pops,
Just like my love for donuts and hops.
With every beat, my belly shakes,
At the sight of cake, my diet breaks!

Romance blooms in butter and toast,
A breakfast feast I love the most.
So here's to love that's slightly absurd,
With whipped cream kisses, oh, how I've stirred!

Join me in giggles where sweetness lies,
In crumbs and laughs, under doughy skies.
With every beat, through thick and thin,
Love's just a pastry, let the fun begin!

Resonance of Nature's Pulse

Amidst the trees, a squirrel just swung,
He stole my snack; he's like Tarzan, sprung!
With acorns flying, a furry thief,
In woods of laughter, he's the chief!

Oh, frogs croak tunes, like crooners at night,
Their off-key jams cause quite fright.
Yet in their chorus, a symphony swells,
A nature jam where every beast yells!

The flowers dance with a breeze so bold,
Wearing clashing outfits, colors uncontrolled.
Who knew they'd host a rave so raw?
With bees as DJs, we all say, "More!"

Nature chuckles in colors and sounds,
A joyful surprise where silliness abounds.
So if you hear woodland giggles take flight,
Join the fun, dance under moonlight!

Lush Canopies of Being

In a forest lush where the critters roam,
A raccoon wearing shades found a new home.
He struts like a star, oh, such a sight!
A furry rockstar in the soft moonlight.

The trees sway gently, like dancers they twirl,
Each leaf a laugh, in a dash, they whirl.
With roots in gossip, they giggle away,
Sharing tales of squirrels playing ballet!

Under canopies thick, where mischief is rife,
A hedgehog's escape turned into pure life.
He rolled down a hill, a mud ball of fun,
Laughing at clouds as they burst out the sun!

So come join the creatures in this joyous spree,
Celebrate life with a nutty jubilee.
In lush canopies where laughter brings cheer,
In nature's embrace, let's hold love dear!

Wisps of Inner Fire

In my soul, a spark prances around,
A wisp of joy, where giggles abound.
It tickles my heart like a featherlight breeze,
Turning my frowns into snorts of ease.

With coffee in hand, I march like a king,
Each sip a tune that makes my heart sing.
Come join the party, the caffeine brigade,
With jumpy legs, on this wild parade!

Together we dance, with cups held high,
When laughter erupts, it reaches the sky.
A fire within keeps the silliness near,
With wisdom wrapped in a can of beer!

So let's fuel the flame with quirky delight,
In this blithe chaos, everything feels right.
With wisps of joy lighting up the night,
Join the bonfire; let's get ignited!

The Language of Leaves

Leaves chatter softly, a gossiping crew,
Whispering secrets, while swaying anew.
They giggle at squirrels, who fumble and fall,
And chuckle at raindrops, who splatter and sprawl.

With every rustle, they share tales of jest,
Of branches that tickle, and roots that invest.
A leaf on the breeze, a ticklish delight,
In nature's own language, all laughter takes flight.

Cradle of Courage

In the heart of the forest, a dreamer takes stand,
With daisies for armor and pinecone in hand.
Frogs laugh in chorus, with marbles they play,
While beetles in capes plot the great hero's way.

A brave little chipmunk, with attitude bold,
Challenges shadows, both timid and old.
He leaps over puddles, claiming each drop,
In the cradle of courage, he'll never stop!

Reflections in the Dew

Dewdrops hang laughing on leaves like a prank,
Each one a tiny mirror, a splash of a prank.
They catch the sun's glimmer, a disco ball glow,
While ants throw a rave, in line and in row.

As morning approaches, the music gets loud,
With crickets as DJs, they draw in a crowd.
They dance in the light, like no one will see,
In reflections of dew, they're completely carefree!

Journey Through the Verdant

A snail on a mission, with purpose and flair,
Takes slow tiny steps, through bushes and air.
It glides past a bug who's stuck in a funk,
And shares all the gossip of flowers and junk.

The journey is wobbly, but laughs fill the gap,
As they trip on a twig, or nap on a map.
Through the green-covered land, with friends who all cheer,
Each step is a treasure, each giggle sincere.

Gossamer Dreams

In the land of floating socks,
Where laughter grows in silken rocks,
The gnomes all dance with fluffy sheep,
And tickle clouds while we all sleep.

Chasing butterflies with zest,
While giggling bugs just take a rest,
The cupcakes bounce upon the beam,
In this realm of silly dreams.

We ride on waves of jelly beans,
With peanut butter kings and queens,
Each hiccup sprouts a silly song,
In a world where nothing's wrong.

Hooray for socks that fly and twist,
In dreams where nothing can be missed,
With sugar sprinkles in the air,
Join the frolic, if you dare!

Nature's Lullaby

The trees hum tunes of olden days,
As squirrels hold brass and laugh in plays,
A sunbeam tickles every leaf,
While shadows dance with snowball grief.

The rivers giggle, oh what a sight,
As frogs in bow ties leap in fright,
Butterflies wear hats too big,
In the orchestra of a bouncing jig.

The flowers sing with voices sweet,
As daisies tap their tiny feet,
The wind tells jokes that make us smile,
While ants all march in single file.

Nature jokes and dances too,
In magic moments, bright and blue,
With every tickle, laugh, and sigh,
Life's a jest under the sky!

Harmonies in Hues

In the palette where laughter blooms,
Colors dance inside their rooms,
The oranges giggle, reds take flight,
While violets whisper, 'Is it night?'

The blues wear shoes that squeak and shout,
As greens prance round, there's never doubt,
Each canvas winks with every hue,
In mirthful glee, they paint anew.

Dancing brushes hop and sway,
Creating joy in every way,
With every stroke, a chuckle grows,
Where every color truly glows.

So bring your brush, don't stand aside,
In this symphony, come and glide,
For in each tone, a chuckle brews,
In harmonies of wondrous views!

Tides of Tranquility

The waves wear hats that flip and flop,
As dolphins at the surf just stop,
In tides of giggles rolling in,
Splashing joy where laughter's been.

Seashells whisper jokes to sand,
While crabs all tap to make a band,
The buoyant breeze just whoops and cheers,
As nature bands its giggly gears.

The sunlight dances on the shore,
While seagulls shout, 'Don't be a bore!'
With every wave, a chuckle swirls,
Welcoming in the joy of pearls.

So let the ocean's laughter flow,
In every wave, there's room to grow,
With every tide, a whimsy ride,
In tranquil bliss where jokes abide!

A Canopy of Dreams

Under the shade of a teapot tree,
We sip our thoughts, feel quite carefree.
The squirrels wear hats, oh what a sight,
As they dance and giggle in morning light.

Beneath the branches, we play charades,
With friendly frogs in silly parades.
A breeze blows laughter, we can't stay still,
Join the fun, it's a whimsical thrill!

The clouds roll by, with faces we know,
With goofy smiles, they put on a show.
We twirl and spin, catch giggles on air,
In this canopy, there's magic to share.

So lift your cup to clouds up above,
Where dreams grow wild, and spirits dance with love.
In this funny place, we'll laugh till we swoon,
Beneath the shade of a delightful moon.

Celestial Roots in the Earth

Deep in the soil where gnomes dig deep,
Dance with the roots while the fairies sleep.
A cabbage with glasses reads the news,
While carrots gossip and gossip ensues.

The moon plays cards with a wobbly sun,
While crickets cheer, oh what goofy fun!
The daisies giggle, they bloom in a fuss,
Let's join the laughter, no need to rush!

Fungi wear coats, oh what a sight,
Juggling raindrops in the soft twilight.
The worms provide music, a jazzy night,
With roots that twist in a laughable plight.

So let's dig deep, where the humor grows,
In earthy antics, our friendship flows.
For under our feet, a circus thrives,
In the joyful soil, where wisdom jives.

Whispering Blooms of Intent

In a garden of giggles, the blooms converse,
Sharing secrets so funny, I couldn't rehearse.
A tulip in pink tries to tell a joke,
While roses are rolling, they're tickled and choked.

The daisies join in with their silly puns,
While lilies wear shoes, oh, aren't they fun?
Butterflies flutter, then slip on a slide,
In this bloom-filled world, we jubilantly glide.

A bumblebee buzzes, with tales of delight,
Of flowers who dance in the moon's soft light.
Petals in laughter tip-toe on air,
In a whispering symphony, humor we share.

So join the party where giggles abound,
Among blooms of joy that dance round and round.
In gardens so vivid, let's laugh and ascend,
With whispers of nature that never quite end.

Unfurling Dreams of Tomorrow

In the morning dew, our dreams unfurl,
A pancake-sun gives the day a twirl.
With toast in hand, we're ready to fly,
Like pancakes soaring up high in the sky.

A dandelion whispers, "Let's blow and roam!"
While giggling clouds invite us back home.
The wind wears a cape and does a soft twirl,
In this zany space, our laughter will whirl.

With socks on our heads, we skip down the lane,
In a world full of silly, it's perfectly sane.
Bouncing along, on sprightly old feet,
As we tumble and giggle, life feels so sweet.

So let's dream aloud with each hearty cheer,
Embracing the funny, let go of all fear.
For tomorrows are bright, with laughter we sow,
In this garden of humor, let happiness grow!

Ferns in the Twilight

Ferns giggle in the dusk,
They tickle toes and blush.
Whispers of green prance around,
In this twilight, joy is found.

Mushrooms wear a party hat,
While crickets dance on a mat.
A ladybug does the cha-cha,
In this leafy dual gala.

Stars peek from the deep blue sky,
As each leaf waves its goodbye.
Silly shadows start to play,
Twilight's mischief on display.

In this space of whimsy bright,
Ferns twirl with pure delight.
Who knew nature had such flair?
Join the fun without a care!

Echoing Through the Garden

Bunnies hide in leafy beds,
Playing tag with their tiny heads.
Garden gnomes hold secret chats,
In shrubby coats and pointy hats.

Daisies don a flower crown,
While sunflowers twirl around.
Carrots giggle underground,
As they bounce with joyful sound.

A squirrel juggles acorns high,
With the birds cheering nearby.
Echoes of laughter ringing clear,
Nature's fun is always near.

Butterflies wearing silly socks,
Flap along like quirky clocks.
Whimsy dances in the breeze,
In this garden, hearts find ease!

Buds of Transformation

Tiny buds with curious grins,
Dream of where this journey begins.
They pop open with a cheer,
Transforming life from year to year.

Caterpillars munch and laugh,
Finding joy in their green path.
Chrysalis, a cozy place,
For surprising change to embrace.

When the blooms burst through the day,
They show off in a bold display.
Colors splatter through the air,
Nature's art beyond compare.

In this cycle filled with glee,
Life's a dance, as it should be.
From timid buds to vibrant bloom,
A funny tale in every room!

Ribbons of Celestial Light

Stars throw parties in the night,
Wearing ribbons oh so bright.
Moonbeams giggle, twirl, and spin,
Lighting up the world within.

The comets race with flashy tails,
While space dust tells funny tales.
Galaxies swirl in vibrant hues,
Under influences from cosmic blues.

Nebulas dressed up in style,
Flash their colors with a smile.
Asteroids play a game of tag,
In this vast and joyful rag.

Each twinkle sings a silly song,
In this cosmos, we all belong.
Ribbons twine in playful flight,
Crafting dreams under starlit night!

Vertical Journeys of Heart and Soil

In gardens where the daisies prance,
The worms do a wiggly dance.
They twirl and spin in gentle glee,
Declaring, "Look! We're fashionably free!"

With roots that tickle beneath the ground,
They whisper secrets all around.
The carrots giggle in bright orange coats,
While celery styles its leafy floats.

The daisies keep their heads held high,
While beets in red, politely sigh.
"Why must we stay when dreams are vast?
Let's climb and surf! A blast from the past!"

Yet soil gives hugs that last and cling,
And who would trade such a cozy ring?
For laughter in the dirt we find,
Is worth more than a carefree mind.

Tides of Spirit and Blossom

Bumblebees wear tiny frowns,
As they bump into flowers around.
"Excuse me, pardon, oh dear me!"
Said the bee, while sipping tea.

The flowers giggle, petals in flight,
"Oh buzz off, it's a fine day bright!"
Cherry blossoms laugh with a pink-tipped tease,
As dandelions roll in the gentle breeze.

A tulip sways with a knowing grin,
"We're all here just to dive right in!"
The daisies erupt in a boisterous song,
While the sun smiles down and hums along.

But as the tide pulls life back home,
The flowers chuckle, they need not roam.
For every bloom brings a cheer so sweet,
In nature's punchline, we find our beat.

Rooted in the Infinite

In the garden of giggles, roots intertwine,
Where the lettuce pranks all in straight lines.
"Can you believe we are stuck down here?"
Asked the radish, blushing, full of cheer.

Pumpkins roll with laughter, feeling spry,
While squash jokes about growing exceedingly high.
"Who needs to climb when we can just root?"
Laughed the turnip, sporting a funny suit.

As the beetroot chuckles, it blushes bright,
Underneath the soil, it feels just right.
They've built a world of humor and jest,
For what could be better than being a guest?

Digging deep and cracking wise,
In this fun-laden earth, the laughter flies.
For every giggle echoes, you see,
In the heart of dirt, we're all truly free.

Shadows Cast by Sunlight

Beneath the sun, the shadows play,
Making faces throughout the day.
The sunflowers stretch, so tall and proud,
While nearby peas whisper to the crowd.

"Look at my shade, it's dapper and grand!"
Said the beet, tipping a leafy hand.
The broccoli, jolly, waved in reply,
"Your shadow sings, oh my, oh my!"

Chlorophyll laughter fills the air,
As cilantro twirls without a care.
With funky dances and sun-kissed cheer,
Every shadow holds a friend near.

Through sunlight's love, the giggles bloom,
While shadows cast away all gloom.
For in the garden, this jesters' spree,
Makes every shade as bright as can be.

www.ingramcontent.com/pod-product-compliance
Lightning Source LLC
Chambersburg PA
CBHW051640160426
43209CB00004B/724